GREAT CAREERS IN
HEALTH CARE

by Meg Gaertner

WWW.FOCUSREADERS.COM

Focus Readers is distributed by North Star Editions:
sales@northstareditions.com | 888-417-0195

Produced for Focus Readers by Red Line Editorial.

Photographs ©: Shutterstock Images, cover, 1, 4–5, 7, 8–9, 11, 13, 15, 16–17, 19, 21, 22–23, 25, 26–27; Red Line Editorial, 29

Library of Congress Cataloging-in-Publication Data
Names: Gaertner, Meg, author.
Title: Great careers in health care / by Meg Gaertner.
Description: Lake Elmo, MN : Focus Readers, [2022] | Series: Great careers | Includes index. | Audience: Grades 4-6
Identifiers: LCCN 2020057986 (print) | LCCN 2020057987 (ebook) | ISBN 9781644938447 (hardcover) | ISBN 9781644938904 (paperback) | ISBN 9781644939369 (ebook) | ISBN 9781644939789 (pdf)
Subjects: LCSH: Allied health personnel--Vocational guidance--United States--Juvenile literature. | Medical care--Vocational guidance--United States--Juvenile literature.
Classification: LCC R697.A4 G34 2022 (print) | LCC R697.A4 (ebook) | DDC 610.73/7069023--dc23
LC record available at https://lccn.loc.gov/2020057986
LC ebook record available at https://lccn.loc.gov/2020057987

Printed in the United States of America
Mankato, MN
082021

ABOUT THE AUTHOR

Meg Gaertner is a children's book writer and editor. She loves learning about advances made in science, medicine, and engineering. When not writing, editing, or learning, she can be found swing dancing or hiking the forests of Minnesota.

TABLE OF CONTENTS

CHAPTER 1

HEALTH CARE

Health care is a growing field. In the United States, experts expect 2.4 million new health-care jobs to be created by 2029. That is a 15 percent increase from 2019. Health care includes many job options. People might first think of **primary care** doctors and nurses. But there are hundreds of **specialties** within

Many nurses work in hospitals. Others work in clinics, schools, and assisted living centers.

medicine. And there are many different kinds of nurses.

Doctors and nurses are not the only people in health care. Allied-health workers also provide care. Some focus on

MEDICINE AND NURSING

Many people consider medicine and nursing to be separate fields. Medicine focuses on preventing and treating health problems. Nursing focuses on providing care to patients. Over the years, the two fields have started to overlap. But there are still differences. Doctors practice medicine by making treatment plans for patients. Nurses carry out those plans. In general, nurses spend more time with patients. They are usually the first health-care workers that patients see.

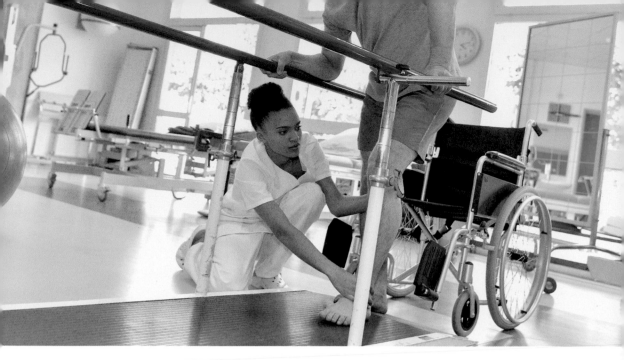

A physical therapist helps a patient regain the ability to walk.

preventing illness and injury. Others help people recover from illness and injury.

Health care also includes jobs in **research** and public health. Some people study the human body. Others focus on the health of groups of people. Overall, jobs in health care have goals of improving health and wellness.

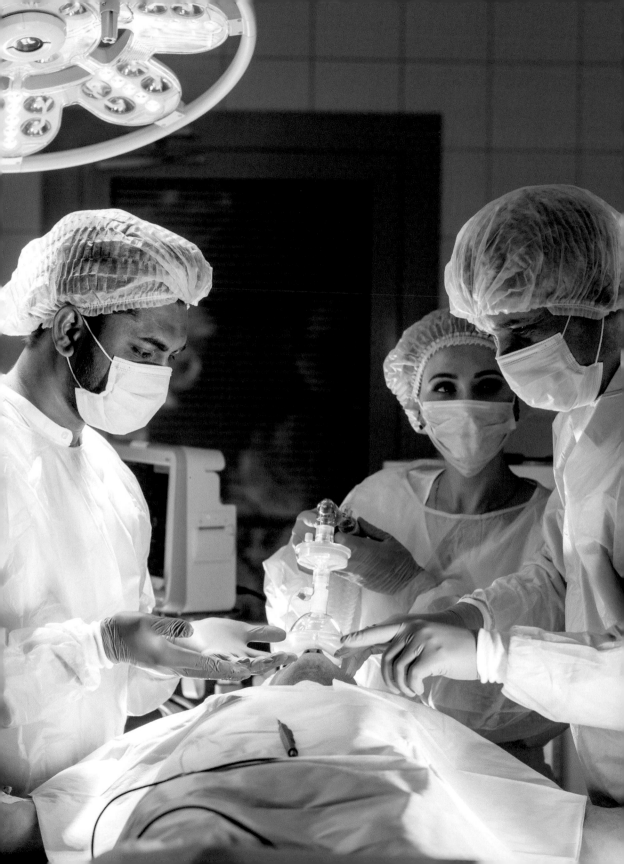

CHAPTER 2

MEDICINE AND NURSING

The human body is very complex. It has many systems and parts. So, doctors often specialize. They focus on one part of the body. They become experts on the diseases affecting that area. For example, some doctors focus on the heart. Some study blood. Others study the lungs and breathing.

Surgeons are doctors who perform operations to repair or remove certain body parts.

Whatever their focus, doctors see people who are having health problems. They listen to people's concerns. Doctors might order lab tests or scans. These tests help doctors understand what is wrong. Then doctors make a **diagnosis**.

PSYCHIATRY

Psychiatrists are medical doctors. Like other doctors, they diagnose and treat patients. But psychiatrists specialize in mental illness. Mental illnesses affect how people think, feel, and act. Mental illness is quite common. One in six young people in the United States experiences a mental illness. Psychiatrists talk with people. They help people choose healthier behaviors. They might also give people medication.

Psychiatrists help patients with mental illness, which affects 20 percent of US adults.

They also suggest treatment options. Treatment might include medication. It might involve changes to a person's eating. It might involve **surgery**.

Surgeons specialize in doing surgery. Some of these doctors are skilled at specific surgeries. For example, some might do brain surgery. Others might focus on bones and joints.

Some doctors work to prevent injury. For instance, doctors in sports medicine help athletes exercise safely. Other doctors support people with long-term health conditions. They help manage patients' pain. They might also provide tools such as wheelchairs or **prostheses**. These tools can help some patients be active. The aim of care is to help patients meet their own goals.

All of these doctors are assisted by nurses. Like doctors, nurses have many specialties to choose from. Some nurses aid in surgeries. Others work in doctors' offices. Some nurses work mostly with older people. Some help people manage long-term illnesses. Others work mostly with women during childbirth. Some nurses work with children and teens. These nurses also teach parents how to care for their children's health.

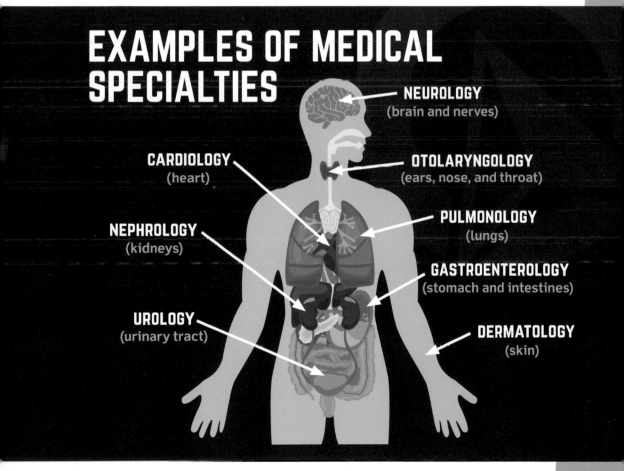

EXAMPLES OF MEDICAL SPECIALTIES

NEUROLOGY
(brain and nerves)

CARDIOLOGY
(heart)

OTOLARYNGOLOGY
(ears, nose, and throat)

PULMONOLOGY
(lungs)

NEPHROLOGY
(kidneys)

GASTROENTEROLOGY
(stomach and intestines)

UROLOGY
(urinary tract)

DERMATOLOGY
(skin)

DIAGNOSTICS

Diagnostics is the process of figuring out what is wrong with a patient. It is a key step in medicine. All doctors want to figure out why their patients feel unwell. But some doctors specialize in this step. Other doctors come to them for help in diagnosing patients.

For example, radiologists use scans to see inside patients' bodies. These scans include X-rays and CT scans. Each test creates images of inside the body. And each test allows radiologists to see different things. X-rays show the patient's bones. CT scans can show **soft tissues**.

Radiologists look at the images. They find the health problem. Then they give this information to a patient's main doctor.

Doctors might also go to pathologists for help. Pathologists take samples of patients' blood,

A radiologist studies images of the patient's body to determine the health problem.

urine, or tissue. They study these samples in lab tests. These tests help pathologists find the cause of a disease.

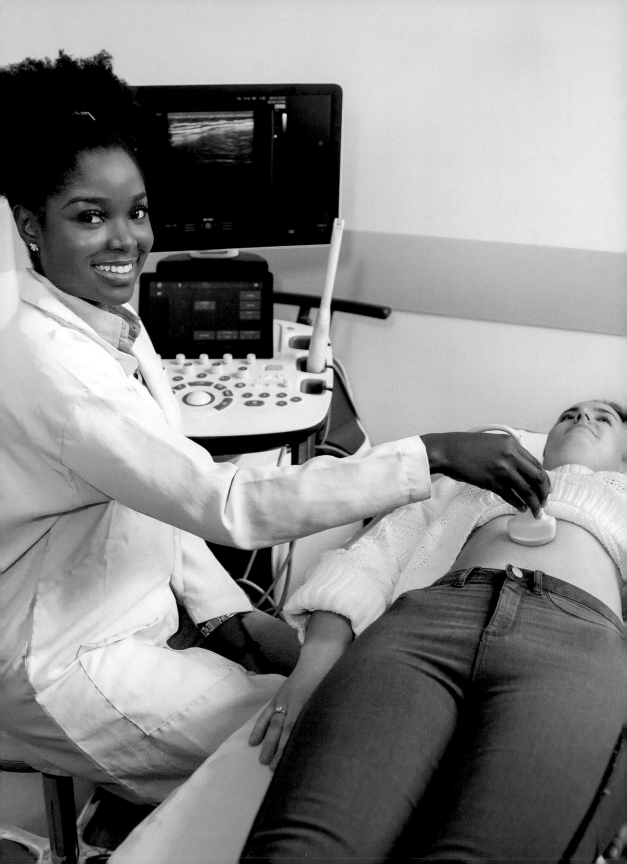

CHAPTER 3

ALLIED HEALTH

Allied health is an important part of health care. It includes all workers beyond doctors, nurses, dentists, and **pharmacists**. Approximately 60 percent of health-care workers are in allied health. They treat and prevent problems. They teach people about wellness. And they help manage the health-care system.

A sonographer operates a machine that uses sound waves to create images of the body.

There are dozens of jobs in allied health. Some people work with machines or tools. They help doctors by running tests and scans. They may also aid during surgeries. Other people specialize in processes such as talking or hearing. They support patients who struggle in these areas.

Allied-health workers can focus on food or exercise, too. Dieticians help people eat well. They prevent and manage disease through healthy eating. Athletic trainers help people stay active. They also help people recover from injuries.

Some injuries and conditions limit people's ability to move. Or they keep

A speech-language pathologist helps a child improve his pronunciation.

people from doing everyday activities. Physical therapists (PTs) are experts on movement. PTs use exercises and touch. They help patients manage pain. And they help improve patients' ability to move. Occupational therapists (OTs) help build people's life skills. These skills can include cooking, eating, getting dressed, and driving. OTs help people become more independent. And they help people find success at work and school.

MANY KINDS OF THERAPY

Some people struggle to connect with others. Other people have trouble handling their own feelings. Many allied-health workers can help them. These workers talk with patients. They learn about the patients' needs and goals. Then they develop a treatment plan. Some workers use music or writing. These activities can improve wellness. They help people express their feelings in healthy ways. Other workers use activities such as dance or play. They help people build confidence. And they support people in working well with others.

A music therapist helps people express their feelings through music.

Not all allied-health workers see patients. Some work in records. They manage patients' health information. Others work in billing. They make sure people pay for health services. Other workers teach people about health. They create programs and events. They help people make healthy choices.

CHAPTER 4

RESEARCH

Diagnoses and treatments are possible because of medical research. Scientists study the human body to better understand how it works. They study the causes of disease. And they develop treatments and cures.

Certain diseases can spread from human to human. Some scientists

Research scientists help develop new drugs that can improve patients' lives.

identify where a disease started. They work to control its spread. Other scientists develop new medications. They see how drugs affect diseased tissue.

Research and working with patients are both important. Some people want to

PUBLIC HEALTH

Public health focuses on the health of large groups. It aims to prevent disease and injury across populations. The field also studies health differences among groups. Some groups are healthier than others. Researchers aim to learn why. The reasons often have to do with poverty and racism. People don't have equal **access** to clean water, clean air, and healthy food. Public health workers try to reduce these inequalities.

During the COVID-19 pandemic, public health workers set up drive-through testing sites.

do both. They become research doctors. Many of these doctors also teach at universities.

Researchers in health care study more than the human body. Some people study health care itself. They work to lower its costs. And they aim to improve its results. They also work to ensure people have equal access to health care.

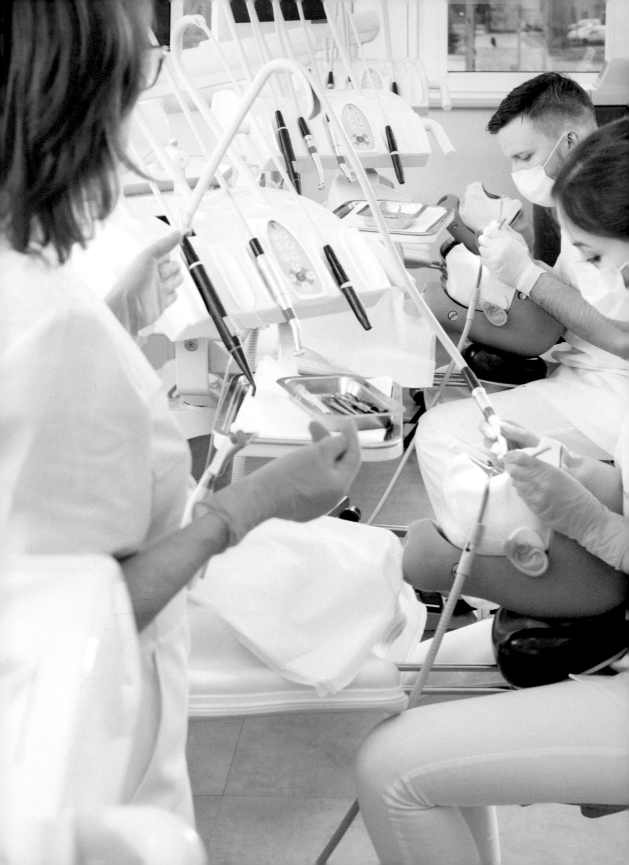

CHAPTER 5

ENTERING THE FIELD

Different jobs in health care require different training. Becoming a medical doctor takes the most time. People first take science classes in college. Then they complete four years of medical school. After that, they spend three to nine years studying a specialty. This study includes hands-on training.

Dentistry students train on dummies to gain practice.

Nursing has many levels. People can become nurses and nurse's aides in less than two years. But more schooling leads to higher pay and more opportunities. And many hospitals and clinics require nurses to have a four-year college degree.

Each allied-health job requires different training. Jobs treating patients typically require a college degree. And some require education beyond college. Jobs working with machines require less schooling. These jobs also offer on-the-job training.

In all health-care jobs, people work together to care for patients. Teamwork is an important skill. From patient care to research, there are many career options. And the jobs are rewarding. Workers know they are helping people. They are serving their communities.

CAREER PREP CHECKLIST

Interested in a career in health care? As you move into middle school and high school, try these steps.

1 Study hard in school. Take math and science classes, including biology, chemistry, and anatomy.

2 Read books on science and healthy living. Ask a librarian for help finding these books.

3 Tell your school's guidance counselor about your interest. This person can help you find opportunities to get experience in health care.

4 At your next checkup, ask the doctor or nurse if you could sit down with them sometime to talk about their work. If they agree, prepare a list of questions for your conversation with them.

5 Some hospitals and clinics have volunteer programs. Ask if you can help out and get experience.

6 See if your area has summer camps or after-school programs in science and health. Use the internet to find these opportunities.

FOCUS ON
GREAT CAREERS IN HEALTH CARE

Write your answers on a separate piece of paper.

1. Write a paragraph explaining the main ideas of Chapter 2.

2. Do you think working with patients or doing research would be more interesting? Why?

3. Approximately what percent of health-care workers are in allied-health roles?

   A. 15 percent
   B. 20 percent
   C. 60 percent

4. Why does it take more schooling to become a doctor than a nurse or an allied-health worker?

   A. Nurses and allied-health workers deal with more complex parts of the body.
   B. It takes more time for doctors to specialize and learn how to make diagnoses.
   C. Doctors have fewer duties than nurses or allied-health workers.

Answer key on page 32.

GLOSSARY

access
The opportunity to use something or benefit from it.

diagnosis
The naming of a patient's illness, disease, or health problem.

pharmacists
People who are experts on medication and help others use medication safely.

primary care
Health care provided by non-emergency workers, often for the most common problems.

prostheses
Artificial body parts.

research
The act of studying something to learn more about it.

soft tissues
Tissues such as fat and muscle that surround, support, and connect other tissues in the body.

specialties
Areas of study that people can become experts in.

surgery
A medical procedure to fix a problem inside the body.

TO LEARN MORE

BOOKS

Alkire, Jessie. *Medicine: From Hippocrates to Jonas Salk.* Minneapolis: Abdo Publishing, 2019.

Hudd, Emily. *Frontline Heroes.* Minneapolis: Abdo Publishing, 2021.

Kurtz, Kevin. *The Future of Medicine.* Minneapolis: Lerner Publications, 2021.

NOTE TO EDUCATORS

Visit **www.focusreaders.com** to find lesson plans, activities, links, and other resources related to this title.

INDEX

Answer Key: 1. Answers will vary; **2.** Answers will vary; **3.** C; **4.** B